REGIONAL WILD AMERICA

S0-BCA-689

UNIQUE ANIMALS OF THE NORTHEAST

By Tanya Lee Stone

BLACKBIRCH PRESS

An imprint of Thomson Gale, a part of The Thomson Corporation

THOMSON

GALE

Detroit • New York • San Francisco • San Diego • New Haven, Conn. • Waterville, Maine • London • Munich

THOMSON
™
GALE

For my unique children of the Northeast—Jake and Liza

Photo Credits: Cover Image: © Robert Y. Ono/CORBIS; © John Conrad/CORBIS, 11, 18; © E.R. Degginger/Photo Researchers, Inc., 21; © Peter Finger/CORBIS, 5; © Darrell Gulin/CORBIS, 3; © Wolfgang Kaehler/CORBIS, 19; © George D. Lepp/CORBIS, 15, 17; © Andrew J. Martinez/Photo Researchers, Inc., 20; © Joe McDonald/CORBIS, 10, 12; © Minden Pictures, 23, 24; © Stan Osolinski/CORBIS, 8; © Lynda Richardson/CORBIS, 9; © D. Robert & Lorri Franz/CORBIS, 6, 7, 13; © Ron Sanford/CORBIS, 17; © Paul A. Souders/CORBIS, 14; © Kennan Ward/CORBIS, 15, 16; Steve Zmina, 4

LIBRARY OF CONGRESS CATALOGING-IN-PUBLICATION DATA

Stone, Tanya Lee.
    Unique animals of the Northeast / by Tanya Lee Stone.
      p. cm. — (Regional wild America)
    Includes bibliographical references and index.
    ISBN 1-56711-966-2 (hard cover: alk. paper)
    1. Animals—Northeastern States—Juvenile literature. I. Title II. Series: Stone, Tanya Lee. Regional wild America.
    QL157.N67S76 2005
    591.974—dc22
                                                          2004013959

Printed in the United States of America
10 9 8 7 6 5 4 3 2 1

Contents

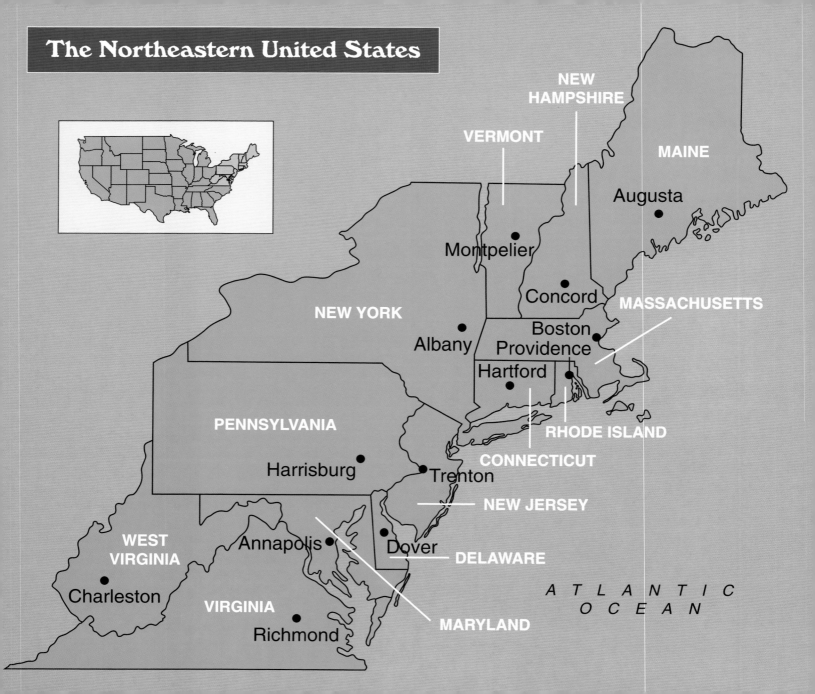

The Northeastern United States

NEW HAMPSHIRE

VERMONT

MAINE

Augusta

Montpelier

Concord

NEW YORK

MASSACHUSETTS

Boston

Albany

Providence

Hartford

PENNSYLVANIA

RHODE ISLAND

CONNECTICUT

Harrisburg

Trenton

NEW JERSEY

WEST VIRGINIA

Annapolis

Dover

DELAWARE

Charleston

VIRGINIA

ATLANTIC OCEAN

Richmond

MARYLAND

Introduction

In the Northeast, birds fly, marine life swims, and animals travel across the land. Many different animals make their homes here. Some animals are especially well known in this region.

The sky glows red over a Maine lighthouse at dawn. The Northeast is home to a variety of animals.

Bouncing Bunnies

The eastern cottontail is a very common sight throughout the Northeast. This grayish-brown rabbit gets its name from its fluffy, white, cottony tail. Cottontails have long ears and large eyes. They have excellent senses of smell, sight, and hearing. Like other rabbits, they have long hind legs for hopping. These rabbits weigh between 2 and 4 pounds (0.9 and 1.8kg) and are about 12 to 18 inches (30 to 46cm) long. They live almost anywhere there is enough brush in which to hide.

Cottontails are herbivores. This means they mainly eat plants. They love clover and graze on different kinds of grasses. They will also eat garden vegetables. These rabbits have many predators (animals that hunt other animals for food). Foxes, hawks, owls, snakes, and many other animals eat rabbits. Humans hunt rabbits, too.

Although rabbits are heavily hunted, there are always plenty of them around. Female cottontails often give birth four or five times a year. Each litter (group of babies) has between two and eight bunnies. The mother makes a nest by digging a shallow hole in the ground and lining it with grass and some fur from her belly. Although the bunnies are born blind, they are able to leave the nest on their own within three to four weeks.

The eastern cottontail is found throughout the Northeast. This herbivore eats grasses and garden vegetables.

Totally Toads!

The American toad is found throughout the Northeast region. This amphibian does well wherever there is moisture and enough insects to eat. It lives in fields, forests, and even backyards. An amphibian is an animal that is able to live both on land and in the water.

A common amphibian of the Northeast, the American toad puffs its throat to make a trilling sound.

Toads have glands near the shoulders that produce poison, so hand washing is a must after handling a toad.

A toad's skin is rough and dry. Toads have short back legs and hop instead of jump. They do not have webbed feet. Although tadpoles (baby toads) live in the water until they change into toads, the adults spend most of their time on land.

Like most toads, the American toad has excellent vision, which helps it find food and protect itself. Its eyes are large and set wide apart. This lets a toad see in all directions. Toads also have a special weapon for defense against predators. Glands near their shoulders produce a poison that will make many kinds of animals sick. For this reason, people should always wash their hands after handling toads.

Groundhogs are sometimes called woodchucks. They are furry, plant-eating rodents that live in tunneled burrows.

Gobbling Groundhogs

Groundhogs, or woodchucks, are rodents and are related to squirrels. They weigh between 5 and 14 pounds (2 and 6kg) and are about 14 to 26 inches (36 to 66cm) long. Groundhogs have short legs and bushy tails. They communicate with other groundhogs by making a variety of noises. They make a loud whistling sound to signal danger. Groundhogs are mainly plant eaters. They eat flowers, herbs, grasses, and leaves. They also disturb people's gardens, gobbling up vegetables such as peas and beans. Groundhogs love apples, which they will climb trees to get. They are good climbers, swimmers, and diggers.

Groundhogs dig burrows that usually have a main entrance and one or more side entrances. Tunnels lead to one main room. Groundhogs escape predators such as wolves and owls by going into their burrows. The burrow is also used for sleeping and nesting. Baby groundhogs are called kits. They are born in the spring. At birth, kits are tiny and helpless. They do not leave the burrow until they are six or seven weeks old.

Groundhogs often hibernate (go into a deep sleep) through the coldest parts of the winter. It is a myth that the end of winter can be told by a groundhog coming out of its burrow and seeing its shadow. But Groundhog Day is still celebrated for fun each year on February 2.

Groundhogs like to eat flowers and will snack on people's garden vegetables.

11

Furry Foxes

The red fox is common throughout the Northeast. These foxes can be silver or gray, but many have rusty-red fur, which gives this animal its name. Its thick fur keeps the fox warm through winter. Its legs are black and it has a bushy white-tipped tail. Foxes are about 2 feet (0.6m) in length. Their long tails add another 14 to 17 inches (36 to 43cm) to their overall length. Red foxes have pointy snouts and large, pointed ears.

Thick fur keeps the red fox warm in winter. These kits wait for their parents in the den.

Foxes are omnivores. This means they eat both plants and animals. In the winter, they rely mainly on rabbits and small rodents such as rats and mice for food. In the summer, they often eat a lot of fruits and insects. They are mostly active at night.

These animals mainly live in open areas, except during breeding times. Baby foxes are called kits or pups. They are born blind and weigh only a few ounces. Foxes dig dens or take over the burrows of other animals—such as groundhogs—to keep their kits safe for the first several weeks of life. Red foxes usually mate for life. Both parents help care for the young.

Black Bears

Black bears live in many parts of North America, but have become more and more common in the Northeast. They like wooded areas where there are plenty of places to hide. Although they generally stay away from people, black bears have gotten used to living near suburbs where people's garbage cans offer a constant food supply.

Black bears are omnivores. In the wild, they eat fish and small mammals. They prefer plant foods such as nuts, fruits, leaves, and grasses. As they eat, they scatter seeds. This helps new plants grow.

Black bears prefer munching on plant foods such as dandelions.

A mother bear closely guards her cub. These black bear cubs at right check each other out by sniffing.

Adult black bears can weigh more than 300 pounds (136kg). Females are smaller and weigh between 100 and 150 pounds (45 and 68kg). These large mammals have small eyes, small round ears, and short tails. Black bears are not only black. Their fur comes in shades of brown, tan, reddish brown, and black.

Marvelous Moose

Moose are found in the forests and swamps of the Northeast. (They also live in Canada, Alaska, and some parts of the Rocky Mountain region.) Moose are the official state animal of Maine. They belong to the deer family. In fact, moose are the largest members of this family. Male moose can weigh up to 1,800 pounds (817kg). That is as much as ten adult men!

Moose are the largest members of the deer family. These big animals are very good swimmers.

Each spring, males grow antlers. Velvet, a fuzzy covering, grows over the antlers. In the fall, the velvet begins to peel off. The male sheds his antlers in the winter. A larger pair will grow the following spring. A male's antlers can span nearly 6 feet (1.8m) from end to end.

Moose are herbivores. They graze on willows and water plants in the warm months. In winter, they eat twigs, buds, and bark. Moose are good swimmers and can run quickly and quietly through the forest. Their long legs help them travel through deep snow. Moose are hunted by wolves, bears, and people.

Each spring, male moose grow a new, bigger pair of antlers.

Dandy Deer

The white-tailed deer is named for its brown tail with white edges and a white underside. These deer flash the white underside of their tail to send a danger signal to other deer. This is called tail flagging. Adult females also flag their tails to lead their baby deer, or fawns, through the forest. A fawn's coat is spotted with white. This helps protect the fawn, because predators can mistake the markings for spots of sunlight in the forest.

The white spots on a fawn's coat help protect it from predators. At right, a female white-tailed deer keeps her fawns close.

The white-tailed deer lives in many parts of the United States. It is a very common sight, though, in the Northeast region. In fact, the white-tailed deer is the state mammal of Pennsylvania. Deer live in meadows and woodlands. They are herbivores. They eat shoots, buds, leaves, and stems. They nibble on nuts and fruit. In winter, deer eat bark and tall brush. They also dig under snow to uncover any food they can find.

Deer are shy, gentle animals. Female deer are called does and males are called bucks. Does and fawns often live and feed together in small groups. Bucks also form small groups of their own. White-tailed deer have excellent senses of sight, smell, and hearing. They use these senses to tell when a threat is near. Deer are swift runners and move quickly to escape danger.

Crustaceous Critters!

The Northeast is home to two crustaceans—blue crabs and lobsters—that regularly end up on dinner plates! A crustacean is a marine animal with an exoskeleton (its shell) and a jointed body. Blue crabs are good hunters. They eat other crabs, clams, snails, dead or live fish, and marine plants. Some parts of this crab's body are blue. It has four sets of legs—three for walking and a fourth, paddle-shaped pair for swimming. Females only mate once in their lives. But they deposit between 2 and 8 million eggs into the water!

A lobster (left) and blue crab (right) both have exoskeletons (their shells).

Blue crabs swim off the eastern coast. They are especially high in numbers in the slightly salty waters of Chesapeake Bay. Blue crabs are the Maryland state crustacean. Many people work as crab catchers for the fishing industry.

In Maine and Massachusetts, people make a living catching lobsters and selling them. Like blue crabs, lobsters are good hunters and will eat almost anything they can find. Favorite foods include crabs, clams, mussels, worms, and sea urchins. A lobster's large front claws are used for grabbing and crushing prey (animals that are hunted for food). Blue crabs and lobsters both share a main predator in common, too—human beings!

Whopping Whale!

The commercial hunting of the northern right whale has been illegal for more than one hundred years. Even so, there are only several hundred of these mammals left worldwide. Today, the northern right whale is an endangered animal. It is also the state marine mammal of Massachusetts. This whale swims in the waters off the eastern coast.

Northern right whales like to breach, or jump out of the water. Here, a northern right's tail is seen as the whale dives back under the surface.

These large whales weigh more than 200,000 pounds (90,800kg). They can stretch more than 60 feet (18m) in length. Northern right whales are very slow swimmers, reaching speeds of only about 6 miles (10km) per hour. This made them an easy target for human hunters. In fact, this whale got its common name from fishermen who called it the "right" whale to hunt.

Northern right whales are one of four kinds of baleen whales. Instead of teeth, these whales have big, brushy plates in their mouth called baleen. To feed, the whale opens its mouth, and water and food flood in. But as the water flows back out, the baleen acts like a strainer and catches the food. These huge animals mainly eat tiny shrimplike animals called krill.

There are many unique and wonderful animals that live in the Northeast. All of them add to the richness and beauty of this region.

Glossary

Baleen Large, brushlike structures in a baleen whale's mouth.
Herbivore An animal that mainly eats plants.
Omnivore An animal that eats plants and other animals.

Predator An animal that hunts another animal for food.
Prey An animal that is hunted by another animal.

For More Information

Barrett, Jalma, *Foxes*. San Diego, CA: Blackbirch Press, 2003.

Jacobs, Lee, *Deer*. San Diego, CA: Blackbirch Press, 2003.

Tanya Lee Stone, *Living in a World of Blue: Where Survival Means Blending In*. San Diego, CA: Blackbirch Press, 2001.

Nathalie Ward, *Do Whales Ever…?* Camden, ME: Down East, 1997.

Index